ROB DE JONGH

Joshua

Food for thought in the Old Testament series

Scripture quotations from the Authorized (King James) Version. Rights in the Authorized Version in the United Kingdom are vested in the Crown. Reproduced by permission of the Crown's patentee, Cambridge University Press.

Contributions by Peter L. Forbes used by kind permission.

First edition

ISBN: 978-1-913699-00-0

This book was professionally typeset on Reedsy. Find out more at reedsy.com

To Peter, whose example and confidence in me allowed me to start writing.

Contents

Introduction   iv

   Reading with your family   v

   Leading discussion groups   v

   Preparing a Bible talk or lecture   v

   Preparing a sermon or exhortation   vi

   Aiding personal Bible study   vi

   How not to use this book!   vi

Food for thought in Joshua   viii

Joshua 1   1

   The humble servant   1

Joshua 2   4

   Would you have chosen Rahab?   4

Joshua 3   6

   The miraculous Jordan River and Red Sea crossings   6

Joshua 4   9

   The twelve stones   9

Joshua 5   12

   How God protected Israel's incapacitated fighting men 12

Joshua 6   15

   A woman worth more than gold   15

Joshua 7   18

   The brother who drew near and the brother who
   drew back   18

Joshua 8   22

   Hidden leader, hidden city   22

Joshua's knowledge of the Law   23
Joshua 9   26
  The Gibeonites and Jesus's parables   26
  The Gibeonite model of salvation by faith   27
Joshua 10   31
  How the Gibeonites inadvertently helped Joshua
  conquer the land   31
Joshua 11   34
  Would you live as a dog or die as a lion?   34
Joshua 12   36
  Little kings and BIG kings   36
Joshua 13   38
  It's fine for us, but can it become a snare to our children?   38
Joshua 14   41
  The LORD is with us: fear them not   41
  Having faith that God is bigger than giants   42
Joshua 15   44
  Once upon a time there were three giants...   44
Joshua 16   46
  Ignoring one small verse of scripture brings gener-
  ations of repercussions   46
Joshua 17   50
  Can jealousy take generations to surface?   50
Joshua 18   53
  Big brothers protecting their little brother   53
Joshua 19   55
  Zorah and Eshtaol   55
Joshua 20   57
  Caleb's dwindling inheritance   57
Joshua 21   60
  Caleb's heir   60

Joshua 22   63
  Assuming the worst intentions   63
  Sharing the spoil   64
Joshua 23   66
  Do only the good bits of the Bible apply to you?   66
  One man shall chase a thousand   67
Joshua 24   71
  Crossing over the flood: Starting a new life   71
Epilogue   73
Other books in the series   74
Index   76
About the Author   93

Introduction

When Jesus taught us to pray "give us today our daily bread", he wasn't talking about food, but the word of God. He said:

Man shall not live by bread alone, but by every word of God.

When Jesus met Peter after his resurrection and told Peter to feed the believers, he didn't mean with fish, but with the word of God:

So when they had dined, Jesus saith to Simon Peter, Simon, son of Jonas, lovest thou me more than these? He saith unto him, Yea, Lord; thou knowest that I love thee. He saith unto him, Feed my lambs.

To find time to read the word of God can be difficult, and to teach it to others can seem an impossible task. Many of us simply *find ourselves* teaching the Bible, either at home to our life partner, or to our children, or as lay teachers or ministers or group leaders, without any training or resources.

Using the *Food for Thought in the Old Testament* series gives you a framework of Bible thoughts for each chapter of the Bible, allowing you to start discussion, create Bible talks and sermons, or simply to meditate on or dig deeper in your own study.

Reading with your family

If you are reading a chapter of the Bible at home with your family, first choose a chapter and read it together, preferably reading out loud (perhaps in sections of 2, 5 or 10 verses each) so that everyone gets a chance to join in. You can then find the relevant chapter in *Food for Thought in Joshua* and read one or more of the thoughts for that chapter. When you encounter a Bible reference, ask someone to turn it up and read it. Once you have finished, there may be questions in the text to answer, or the passage may have provided *food for thought* for further discussion.

Leading discussion groups

If you are leading a Bible discussion group, you could start by reading a chapter of the Bible around the group, followed by your presenting a short introduction of the chapter based on the relevant section of *Food for Thought in Joshua*. Once that is done, open up the group for discussion about any topics raised by the Bible chapter or in your introductory thoughts.

Preparing a Bible talk or lecture

If you are preparing a Bible talk or lecture, *Food for Thought in Joshua* can be used to piece your talk together using several sections of the book, or several books in the series. For example, for a character study on Rahab, use the eBook search feature or paperback index to list any sections including references to "Rahab". In the paperback, for example, you would look at pages 11-12 and 25-26. Piece together any sections that you think go well together, then read those sections and follow the Bible references in your Bible. Finally, put your discoveries down in your own words and practice at least once before presenting them.

Preparing a sermon or exhortation

For a talk/sermon or more motivational style thought, start with a topic
from the contents list at the start of the book or from the index. Focus
on the personal questions thrown up by that section, and spend time
exploring what the Bible characters in that section were feeling, based
on what we are told in the Bible chapter and any references provided in
this book. Read out plenty of scripture during your talk to illuminate
what that character was like and what they went through.

Aiding personal Bible study

For your own personal Bible study, it is often helpful to start somewhere
(anywhere is better than nowhere!) and follow where the path leads.
Food for Thought in Joshua can help with this by providing many links to
related Bible passages. Any of these will be well worth looking at to see
how they relate to the partner passage in Joshua. Once you have two
or more related passages, read over the context of each in your Bible
and see what questions and conclusions jump out. Now follow other
referenced passages out of those chapters, and so on.

How not to use this book!

This book series is not an explanation of the whole Old Testament. To
do that would take a million pages. Many people have foolishly tried
to create books like that, and failed. Reference works on the Bible are
seldomly productive for Bible students, since they can stifle your ability
to read the Word and make your own conclusions based on what you
read.

Remember what we started the introduction with? The Bible is for food, not just for knowledge. Jesus asked Peter to feed, not people, but lambs and sheep. In other words, the Bible text is to be eaten, chewed over, and meditated on, in a similar way to how sheep chew over their food.

Rumination is the key to understanding the Old Testament.

This book is a collection of starting points, one or more for each chapter of Joshua. May God bless you as you step off from these onto your own journey through the scriptures.

Food for thought in Joshua

The book of Joshua begins at the end of Moses's life, with the handover of the responsibility for the children of Israel to Moses's servant, Joshua.

All this time Joshua has been the one quietly working in the background, learning from the great man. How is he now going to garner the respect of the people?

And now that they are finally poised to enter the promised land, who is going to step forward to lead the battle?

We meet characters like Caleb and Rahab, full of faith and desire to serve God. We meet rogues like Achan the "troubler of Israel" and Og, the "last of the giants".

The book of Joshua is truly memorable in its exciting battles, vivid characters, and the questions it asks of us. Will we and our households serve the Lord as Joshua promised to do? Will we be saved in the last days in a similar manner to how Rahab was saved? And will we remain faithful to the end as they did?

The book of Joshua finishes by coming back full circle to the start of Israel's journey from Egypt, carrying the bones of Joseph which he had requested they take for burial in the land. It is that act that is listed in Hebrews 11 as being Joseph's most memorable act of faith. And now having gained their place in the land the Israelites finally lay Joseph to rest, as a testament to the fulfilment of God's promise to Abraham:

And he said unto Abram, Know of a surety that thy seed shall be a stranger in a land that is not theirs, and shall serve them; and they shall afflict them four hundred years; And also that nation, whom they shall serve, will I judge: and afterward shall they come out with great substance. And thou shalt go to thy fathers in peace; thou shalt be buried in a good old age. **But in the fourth generation they shall come hither again:** *for the iniquity of the Amorites is not yet full.* (Gen 15:13-16)

And this wonderfully shows the beauty of the Bible, that if it is read with the events already written in mind (and the events yet to be written too), you will make your greatest discoveries.

Joshua 1

The humble servant

With the first five books of the Bible having drawn to a close, we open a new chapter with Joshua now taking over from Moses. Joshua was at the very least 50 years old and ready for leadership. Moses was 120 years old when he gave up leadership – and only right at the end of his life.

This raises the question – why didn't Joshua step in and take over from this old man earlier?

Comparing the two men the Bible record says, in effect, "Joshua was Moses' servant. But Moses was God's servant"

> *Now after the death of **Moses the servant of the LORD** it came to pass, that the LORD spake unto **Joshua the son of Nun, Moses' minister**, saying, Moses my servant is dead; now therefore arise, go over this Jordan, thou, and all this people, unto the land which I do give to them, even to the children of Israel. (Jos 1:1-2)*

Do you think that made Joshua feel small? And in the previous chapter comparing and contrasting Moses and Joshua, it says this (my paraphrase of Deut 34:9-12):

1

"Joshua may have been full of the spirit of wisdom... but was nothing compared to Moses who the LORD knew face to face. No-one was ever as great as Moses".

Here's the actual Bible text:

And Joshua the son of Nun was full of the spirit of wisdom; for Moses had laid his hands upon him: and the children of Israel hearkened unto him, and did as the LORD commanded Moses. And there arose not a prophet since in Israel like unto Moses, whom the LORD knew face to face, In all the signs and the wonders, which the LORD sent him to do in the land of Egypt to Pharaoh, and to all his servants, and to all his land, And in all that mighty hand, and in all the great terror which Moses shewed in the sight of all Israel. (Deu 34:9-12)

So Joshua appears to have been a man of unfathomable meekness, loyalty and wisdom. When Korah, Dathan and Abiram rose up against Moses, Joshua didn't join their rebellion even though they were popular with the rest of the people. When his time finally came to lead, though God didn't expect him to be as great as Moses, the blessing of Moses was still his:

*There shall not any man be able to stand before thee all the days of thy life: **as I was with Moses, so I will be with thee:** I will not fail thee, nor forsake thee. (Jos 1:5)*

The same example could be used for us. Though we will never be great like Jesus, If we are meek and follow him, his blessing will be on us too:

Blessed are the meek: for they shall inherit the earth. (Mat 5:5)

He shall glorify me: for he shall receive of mine, and shall shew it unto you. All things that the Father hath are mine: therefore said I, that he shall take of mine, and shall shew it unto you. (Jhn 16:14-15)

To him that overcometh will I grant to sit with me in my throne, even as I also overcame, and am set down with my Father in his throne. (Rev 3:21)

Food for thought

v1 - There is a certain irony in the fact that it was Joshua - whose name had been changed from Oshea - who took Israel into the land whereas the northern kingdom was removed in the reign of Hoshea (see Num 13:16 & 2Kings 17:6).

v3 - The promise that all land that Joshua's foot trod on would be given to him, draws on both Genesis 13:17 and Deuteronomy 11:24

Joshua 2

Would you have chosen Rahab?

Sometimes we tend to treat the Bible as a rule book and forget that the rules applied in the working examples (the people recorded in the Bible) are just as much a part of the Bible as the rules themselves.

Take Rahab for example. She was a prostitute and few of us would condone that kind of behaviour or lifestyle. Even fewer of us would say that God would condone it. Furthermore, the place where she lived, Jericho, was doomed to destruction, meaning that God wanted everything in it destroyed. We could be forgiven for assuming that Rahab was a no hoper:

> And **the city shall be accursed, even it, and all that are therein** to the LORD:

But the verse doesn't end there with the death of Rahab:

> *only Rahab the harlot shall live, she and all that are with her in the house, because she hid the messengers that we sent. (Jos 6:17)*

How do we get round that?

The fact is that Rahab survived, and God blessed her with a husband and children, and from her family line, Jesus appeared. We should perhaps spend some personal study time figuring out why this apparent complete disregard to God's "rules" was perpetrated by the spies, Joshua, and even ratified by God Himself. If we don't, we might be in danger of condemning someone like Rahab if we were to meet them in real life.

Jesus did that study. He came across people of questionable character. It seems that Jesus was more ready to apply the example of Rahab than the scribes and Pharisees were (the ones who read mostly the law, not the examples of how the law was applied). Perhaps we need to dig a little deeper than just the commandments of "thou shalt not...".

Food for thought

v9 - Rahab's "I know" is a consequences of what others had "heard". This is the evidence that she was a woman of faith as Hebrews 11:31 explains.

v21 - Of course Rahab did not know how long it would be before the city of Jericho would be taken by Israel. So it would seem that the scarlet line was tied to her window from the day that the spies gave it to her until the time of the overthrow of the city.

Joshua 3

The miraculous Jordan River and Red Sea crossings

In this chapter there is a second miraculous crossing of water by the Children of Israel. God himself likens this crossing to the famous crossing of the Red Sea:

> For the LORD your God dried up the waters of Jordan from before you, until ye were passed over, as the LORD your God did to the Red sea, which he dried up from before us, until we were gone over: (Jos 4:23)

Notice that the reason for the miracle is also the same as the earlier event:

That all the people of the earth might know the hand of the LORD, that it is mighty: that ye might fear the LORD your God for ever. (Jos 4:24)

Compare that wording to the crossing of the Red Sea in Exodus:

> And I will harden Pharaoh's heart, that he shall follow after them; and I will be honoured upon Pharaoh, and upon all his host; that the Egyptians **may know that I am the LORD**. And they did so.

*... And Israel saw that great work which the LORD did upon the Egyptians: and **the people feared the LORD, and believed the LORD**, and his servant Moses.* (Exo 14:4, 31)

Another reason for this miraculous event of the Jordan crossing was to establish Joshua as leader, so that the people would fear and obey him:

And the LORD said unto Joshua, This day will I begin to magnify thee in the sight of all Israel, that they may know that, as I was with Moses, so I will be with thee. And thou shalt command the priests that bear the ark of the covenant, saying, When ye are come to the brink of the water of Jordan, ye shall stand still in Jordan. (Jos 3:7-8)

Notice that God likened this exaltation of Joshua to the exaltation of Moses:

On that day the LORD magnified Joshua in the sight of all Israel; and they feared him, as they feared Moses, all the days of his life. (Jos 4:14)

This is exactly what had happened at the Red Sea crossing:

Thus Israel saw the great work which the Lord had done in Egypt; so the people feared the Lord, and believed the Lord and His servant Moses. (Exo 14:31)

So God is willing to go to great lengths to establish the authority of His chosen ruler, so that the people fear and obey them. Do you think it's significant that in both of these cases He used water, which we're told is a symbol of baptism?

Moreover, brethren, I would not that ye should be ignorant, how that all our fathers were under the cloud, and all passed through the sea; And were all baptized unto Moses in the cloud and in the sea; (1Co 10:1-2)

Food for thought

v1 - "early in the morning" is when many faithful men began their service to God. In Genesis 22:3 Abraham is one example. The lesson for us is clear. There should be no delay in starting the work of God, even if the task may not always be appealing to us.

v3, 6, 8, 11, 14, 15 - There is great focus on the ark (of the covenant) in this event.

Joshua 4

The twelve stones

Now that the people have safely reached the other side of the Jordan, with the waters standing "as a heap", just as it did with the Red Sea crossing, there was one more task that Joshua wanted them to carry out. Joshua selects several men, and asks them to *go back into the River!*

> *Then Joshua called the twelve men, whom he had prepared of the children of Israel, out of every tribe a man: And Joshua said unto them, Pass over before the ark of the LORD your God into the midst of Jordan, and take ye up every man of you a stone upon his shoulder, according unto the number of the tribes of the children of Israel: (Jos 4:4-5)*

Why would he do this? Twelve men have to take a stone on their shoulder. What for? And why had Joshua needed to *prepare* these men?

In verse 8 we see that they laid the stones on the shore, and then Joshua took other stones from the shore into the midst of the Jordan. The comment is made that they "are there to this day". In other words, they were big stones. Was the preparation of these men perhaps to train them to lift and carry heavy weights?

So what were the stones for?

That this may be a sign among you, that when your children ask their fathers in time to come, saying, What mean ye by these stones? Then ye shall answer them, That the waters of Jordan were cut off before the ark of the covenant of the LORD; when it passed over Jordan, the waters of Jordan were cut off: and these stones shall be for a memorial unto the children of Israel for ever. (Jos 4:6-7)

So at the borders of Israel they would be able to look and see where they had come from, and remember that they had been a slave nation in Egypt, and that God had brought them out from there into a land flowing with milk and honey.

Now I think these stones had another significance; twelve stones were brought out of the water, and twelve placed in it. A transaction had been carried out. And these strong men actually had a bit more carrying to do then we would first think. They took them all the way to Gilgal, where Joshua explains their significance further:

*And those twelve stones, which they took out of Jordan, did Joshua pitch in Gilgal. And he spake unto the children of Israel, saying, When your children shall ask their fathers in time to come, saying, What mean these stones? Then ye shall let your children know, saying, Israel came over this Jordan on dry land. For the LORD your God dried up the waters of Jordan from before you, until ye were passed over, as the LORD your God did to the Red sea, which he dried up from before us, until we were gone over: **That all the people of the earth might know the hand of the LORD, that it is mighty: that ye might fear the LORD your God for ever.***

(Jos 4:20-24)

So the stones in Gilgal were an echo, on dry land, of the stones that were lying in the Jordan. They formed a link between the two places, to remind all people of God's mighty work.

Food for thought

v12-13 - The total men of the two and a half tribes amounted to 136,930 when adding the totals from Numbers 26:7, 18, 34. We see that "about 40,000" passed over:

> *And the children of Reuben, and the children of Gad, and half the tribe of Manasseh, passed over armed before the children of Israel, as Moses spake unto them:* **About forty thousand prepared for war passed over before the LORD unto battle,** *to the plains of Jericho.* (Jos 4:12-13)

So it would appear that a significant number remained on the east of Jordan.

v24 - The focus is that God will be known in the earth. A sentiment repeated by Solomon when he dedicated the temple he had built (1 Kings 8:60)

Joshua 5

How God protected Israel's incapacitated fighting men

The miraculous crossing of the Jordan had the desired effect. The inhabitants of the land were petrified:

> *And it came to pass, when all the kings of the Amorites, which were on the side of Jordan westward, and all the kings of the Canaanites, which were by the sea, heard that the LORD had dried up the waters of Jordan from before the children of Israel, until we were passed over, that their heart melted, neither was there spirit in them any more, because of the children of Israel. (Jos 5:1)*

When it says "their heart melted", it means there was no bravery left in them to muster an army and fight. When we read on we see that there was a specific need for this:

> *At that time the LORD said unto Joshua, Make thee sharp knives, and circumcise again the children of Israel the second time. And Joshua made him sharp knives, and circumcised the children of Israel at the hill of the foreskins. And this is the cause why Joshua*

did circumcise: All the people that came out of Egypt, that were
males, even all the men of war, died in the wilderness by the way,
after they came out of Egypt. (Jos 5:2-4)

Now imagine if all your men of fighting age had just been circumcised?
Wouldn't that leave you totally open to attack? In fact, yes, and this very
eventuality was known in Israel's history.

And unto Hamor and unto Shechem his son hearkened all that
went out of the gate of his city; and every male was circumcised,
all that went out of the gate of his city. And it came to pass on
the third day, when they were sore, that two of the sons of Jacob,
Simeon and Levi, Dinah's brethren, took each man his sword, and
came upon the city boldly, and slew all the males. (Gen 34:24-25)

Here just two men slew all the males in an entire city, such was the
incapacitating effect of being circumcised.

So we can see that God had planned the event of the crossing of the
Jordan to buy Israel time, to keep them safe while they were defenceless.

Food for thought

v9 - So Israel had not kept the covenant of circumcision whilst in the
wilderness. However they had to be circumcised to keep the Passover:

And when a stranger shall sojourn with thee, and will keep the
passover to the LORD, let all his males be circumcised, and then let
him come near and keep it; and he shall be as one that is born in
*the land: **for no uncircumcised person shall eat thereof**. (Exo*
12:48)

13

Do you think this means they failed to keep the passover all those years?

v12 - A major transition took place here. The food of God's provision in the wilderness ceased, and the people were to eat of the produce of the land promised to them, even before they had conquered it and taken it for their inheritance.

Joshua 6

A woman worth more than gold

D id you know that Jericho had become devoted to destruction
as described in the law in Leviticus 27:28-29?

*Notwithstanding no devoted thing, that a man shall
devote unto the LORD of all that he hath, both of man and beast,
and of the field of his possession, shall be sold or redeemed: every
devoted thing is most holy unto the LORD. None devoted, which
shall be devoted of men, shall be redeemed; but shall surely be put
to death. (Lev 27:28-29)*

This meant complete annihilation as a devoted offering to God. But for
some reason the silver, gold, bronze and iron was allowed to remain,
and not only that, something else as well:

*And the city shall be accursed, even it, and all that are therein, to the
LORD: **only Rahab the harlot shall live, she and all that are
with her in the house**, because she hid the messengers that we sent.
And ye, in any wise keep yourselves from the accursed thing, lest ye
make yourselves accursed, when ye take of the accursed thing, and*

*make the camp of Israel a curse, and trouble it. But **all the silver, and gold, and vessels of brass and iron, are consecrated unto the LORD**: they shall come into the treasury of the LORD. (Jos 6:17-19)*

Presumably the metals were allowed to be taken because metal survives fire intact and is even purified by it:

*Only the gold, and the silver, the brass, the iron, the tin, and the lead, **Every thing that may abide the fire, ye shall make it go through the fire, and it shall be clean:** nevertheless it shall be purified with the water of separation: and all that abideth not the fire ye shall make go through the water. (Num 31:22-23)*

So if that was the principle behind the precious metals being saved from Jericho, how about the other things mentioned - even Rahab and her family?

It was not possible (under the law) for Rahab and her family to survive without being killed, now that Jericho had become "devoted to destruction". See the end of the passage quoted earlier:

None devoted, which shall be devoted of men, shall be redeemed; but shall surely be put to death. (Lev 27:29)

So why weren't they killed? I think the answer could be in Proverbs 3:13-18, where God likens a woman of wisdom to gold and silver:

Happy is the man that findeth wisdom, and the man that getteth understanding. For the merchandise of it is better than the merchandise of silver, and the gain thereof than fine gold. She is more precious than rubies: and all the things thou canst desire are not to be compared unto her. Length of days is in her right hand; and in her left hand riches and honour. Her ways are ways of pleasantness, and all her paths are peace. She is a tree of life to them that lay hold upon her: and happy is every one that retaineth her. (Pro 3:13-18)

So the principle of the law *was* applied to Rahab, and we see that Joshua understands that the Law of Moses can be interpreted in this way, substituting people for metals.

And he was right. Rahab's wisdom and faith survived the fire of war. Just as gold is purified in fire, Rahab became an especially faithful and devoted servant of God as we can see from her prominent parentage in the line of David and eventually Jesus (see Matt 1:5-16).

Food for thought

v10 - Battles normally are associated with shouting and noise so Israel marching round the city in silence was quite a change from the 'normal' battle. Israel were to learn that the victory was of God and not down to their own might.

v19 - The metals mentioned specifically are the metals of the image in Daniel 2:32. Jericho symbolised the kingdoms of men.

Joshua 7

The brother who drew near and the brother who drew back

When you think about how many people are mentioned in the Bible, and how small a number of words the Bible really contains, you begin to realise how little is said about each. God is selective with what He tells us because He's making specific, important points for us to learn. So if every word counts in the scriptures, what does God mean by calling Achan "the son of Zerah" in v24?

> And Joshua, and all Israel with him, took **Achan the son of Zerah,** and the silver, and the garment, and the wedge of gold, and his sons, and his daughters, and his oxen, and his asses, and his sheep, and his tent, and all that he had: and they brought them unto the valley of Achor. (Jos 7:24)

In Genesis 38:27-30 we have the tale of twin brothers. As they were being born, one was about to come out first, but drew back (as a result he was named Zerah). The other had been last but struggled to come

18

out first (he was named Perez).

> *And it came to pass in the time of her travail, that, behold, twins were in her womb. And it came to pass, when she travailed, that the one put out his hand: and the midwife took and bound upon his hand a scarlet thread, saying, This came out first. And it came to pass, as he drew back his hand, that, behold, his brother came out: and she said, How hast thou broken forth? this breach be upon thee: therefore his name was called Pharez. And afterward came out his brother, that had the scarlet thread upon his hand: and his name was called Zarah. (Gen 38:27-30)*

So the boy's names are related to this event, that one of them "drew back" and one "broke forth".

In Hebrews we are told that only those who draw near to God will be saved:

> **Let us draw near** *with a true heart in full assurance of faith, having our hearts sprinkled from an evil conscience, and our bodies washed with pure water. (Heb 10:22)*

and those who draw back will be rejected:

> *But we are not of them who **draw back** unto perdition; but of them that believe to the saving of the soul. (Heb 10:39)*

Notice that the rest of the chapter in Hebrews also mentions Achan (the son of Zerah) in detail, so we can be clear that this chapter is a commentary on the birth of these boys.

> *For **if we sin wilfully after that we have received the knowl-***

19

edge of the truth, there remaineth no more sacrifice for sins, But a certain fearful looking for of judgment and fiery indignation, which shall devour the adversaries. **He that despised Moses' law** *died without mercy under two or three witnesses* (Heb 10:26-28)

This is what Achan had done, wilfully despising the commandment not to take anything, and yet still doing it.

So each of the two boys had an important descendant, and they signify one of two paths we can take in life. Zerah's descendant was Achan, the one who drew back from obeying God, at the point of entering the promised land, and received judgement from God. Pharez had a much more obedient descendent:

> *And Judas begat* **Phares** *and Zara of Thamar; and Phares begat Esrom; and Esrom begat Aram; ... And Jacob begat Joseph the husband of Mary,* **of whom was born Jesus**, *who is called Christ.* (Mat 1:3, 16)

If we **draw near** to God in faith we will be accepted, like Jesus the descendant of Perez. If, however, we come to know God and accept Jesus His son, and then **draw back**, we will ultimately perish as Achan the son of Zerah. To turn back from the grace and love of God after having come to accept it, is tantamount to despising God's gift, and His son who died for us:

> *He that despised Moses' law died without mercy under two or three witnesses: Of how much sorer punishment, suppose ye, shall he be thought worthy, who hath trodden under foot the Son of God, and hath counted the blood of the covenant, wherewith he was sanctified, an unholy thing, and hath done despite unto the Spirit of grace?* (Heb 10:28-29)

Food for thought

v3 - "Let not all the people go up" indicates that Israel were looking for an easy life rather than waiting for God to advise them what to do.

v16 - Whilst the selection process was taking place Achan clearly knew that he was the one to blame - unless he had persuaded himself that his behaviour was not sinful. So he must have known that he would be found out, yet he remained silent. How often do we, when our conscience convicts us, remain silent?

Joshua 8

Hidden leader, hidden city

This chapter can get a little hard to follow. It helps to know that verse 12 is just a repeat of verse 9 and verse 4, so there is only one group set up in ambush:

And he commanded them, saying, Behold, ye shall lie in wait against the city, even behind the city: go not very far from the city, but be ye all ready: (Jos 8:4)

Joshua therefore sent them forth: and they went to lie in ambush, and abode between Bethel and Ai, on the west side of Ai: but Joshua lodged that night among the people. (Jos 8:9)

And he took about five thousand men, and set them to lie in ambush between Bethel and Ai, on the west side of the city. (Jos 8:12)

Joshua's knowledge of the Law

And the king of Ai he hanged on a tree until eventide: and as soon as the sun was down, Joshua commanded that they should take his carcase down from the tree, and cast it at the entering of the gate of the city, and raise thereon a great heap of stones, that remaineth unto this day. (Jos 8:29)

The removal of the king of Ai from the tree at evening was to observe the command of God, written in the Law of Moses:

His body shall not remain all night upon the tree, but thou shalt in any wise bury him that day; (for he that is hanged is accursed of God;) that thy land be not defiled, which the LORD thy God giveth thee for an inheritance. (Deu 21:23)

It demonstrates that even in the enthusiasm of a battle victory Joshua ensured that the law was observed. Likewise the building of the altar of whole stones is according to the scriptures:

*Then Joshua built an altar unto the LORD God of Israel in mount Ebal, As Moses the servant of the LORD commanded the children of Israel, **as it is written in the book of the law of Moses, an altar of whole stones**, over which no man hath lift up any iron: and they offered thereon burnt offerings unto the LORD, and sacrificed peace offerings.* (Jos 8:30-31)

Joshua had a full grasp of the law:

*And if thou wilt make me an altar of stone, **thou shalt not build it of hewn stone**: for if thou lift up thy tool upon it, thou hast* *polluted it. (Exo 20:25)*

Questions

Q1) When it says Joshua went down into the valley, do you think he went by himself?

*And when they had set the people, even all the host that was on the north of the city, and their liers in wait on the west of the city, **Joshua went that night into the midst of the valley.** (Jos 8:13)*

Do you think he stayed there all night?

Q2) Note in verse 17 that the inhabitants of Bethel were destroyed too.

And there was not a man left in Ai or Bethel, that went not out after Israel: and they left the city open, and pursued after Israel. (Jos 8:17)

Joshua's men even killed the king of Bethel (Josh 12:16). Yet we don't hear any more about that place, whether they burned it or captured it like Ai. Why is this?

Hint for Question 2. The answer may be in the later capture of Bethel in Judges 1:22-25:

*And the house of Joseph, they also went up against Bethel: and the LORD was with them. And the house of Joseph sent to descry Bethel. (Now the name of the city before was Luz.) And the spies saw a man come forth out of the city, and they said unto him, **Shew us, we pray thee, the entrance into the city**, and we will shew* *thee mercy. And when he shewed them the entrance into the city, they smote the city with the edge of the sword; but they let go the man and all his family.*

Q3) Why did Israel go from Jericho inland to Ai, then miles out of their way North to Mount Ebal and Gerizim?

Answers

Q1) I think he stayed there all night. The implication is from verse 9 in the way it talks about the previous night:

*but Joshua lodged **that night** among the people.*

Q2) The entrance to the city of Bethel was hidden and they didn't even realise it was there!

Q3) They were retracing the steps of Abraham who was promised the land they were now coming to take possession of (Genesis 12:7). See in Genesis 12:6 Shechem (in between Ebal and Gerizim), Gen 12:8 in between Bethel and Ai, and Gen 12:10 to Egypt.

Joshua 9

The Gibeonites and Jesus's parables

I s Jesus thinking of the Gibeonites when he speaks of counting the cost before going to war?

> Or what king, going to make war against another king, sitteth not down first, and consulteth whether he be able with ten thousand to meet him that cometh against him with twenty thousand? Or else, while the other is yet a great way off, he sendeth an ambassage, and desireth conditions of peace. (Luk 14:31-32)

They do seem to be a perfect example of what he is conveying in the parable.

Also, have you noticed that their words in v9-10, 24 are virtually the same as Rahab's? Here are the two side by side – how many similarities can you see?

> And they said unto him, From a very far country thy servants are come because of the name of the LORD thy God: for we have heard the fame of him, and all that he did in Egypt, And all that he did to the two kings of the Amorites, that were beyond Jordan,

to Sihon king of Heshbon, and to Og king of Bashan, which was at Ashtaroth. ... And they answered Joshua, and said, Because it was certainly told thy servants, how that the LORD thy God commanded his servant Moses to give you all the land, and to destroy all the inhabitants of the land from before you, therefore we were sore afraid of our lives because of you, and have done this thing. (Jos 9:9-10, 24)

And she said unto the men, I know that the LORD hath given you the land, and that your terror is fallen upon us, and that all the inhabitants of the land faint because of you. For we have heard how the LORD dried up the water of the Red sea for you, when ye came out of Egypt; and what ye did unto the two kings of the Amorites, that were on the other side Jordan, Sihon and Og, whom ye utterly destroyed. And as soon as we had heard these things, our hearts did melt, neither did there remain any more courage in any man, because of you: for the LORD your God, he is God in heaven above, and in earth beneath. (Jos 2:9-11)

What we have in both these cases is Gentiles who, by giving up, end up joining God's people and gaining life in the process. If Jesus was thinking of these scriptures in this way, is it possible that the parables of the lost sheep, lost coin, and lost son in Luke 15 also relate to the believing Gentiles who would inherit the promises while Israel still disbelieved?

The Gibeonite model of salvation by faith

In Joshua 9:1-2 we see that all the nations in this area recognised the threat Israel posed, and formed a confederacy to try to defeat them:

*And it came to pass, when all the kings which were on this side Jordan, in the hills, and in the valleys, and in all the coasts of the great sea over against Lebanon, the Hittite, and the Amorite, the Canaanite, the Perizzite, the Hivite, and the Jebusite, heard thereof; That **they gathered themselves together, to fight with Joshua and with Israel, with one accord.** (Jos 9:1-2)*

No doubt they asked (and expected) the city of Gibeon to join with them, which is why they were so angry with them when they didn't:

Now it came to pass, when Adonizedek king of Jerusalem had heard how Joshua had taken Ai, and had utterly destroyed it; as he had done to Jericho and her king, so he had done to Ai and her king; and how the inhabitants of Gibeon had made peace with Israel, and were among them; That they feared greatly, because Gibeon was a great city, as one of the royal cities, and because it was greater than Ai, and all the men thereof were mighty. Wherefore Adonizedek king of Jerusalem sent unto Hoham king of Hebron, and unto Piram king of Jarmuth, and unto Japhia king of Lachish, and unto Debir king of Eglon, saying, Come up unto me, and help me, that we may smite Gibeon: for it hath made peace with Joshua and with the children of Israel. Therefore the five kings of the Amorites, the king of Jerusalem, the king of Hebron, the king of Jarmuth, the king of Lachish, the king of Eglon, gathered themselves together, and went up, they and all their hosts, and encamped before Gibeon, and made war against it. (Jos 10:1-5)

This event sets the scene for the Gibeonite story, because we find in the next verses that, rather than join with their brethren and neighbours to fight the invader, they responded in the opposite way, seeking refuge with the enemy.

Seeking refuge with the enemy, against the peer pressure of your family, friends and neighbours, is nearly impossible to do. For a start it's scary to approach an enemy and ask for mercy. Secondly, it hurts ones pride. Thirdly, it will mean lower status, becoming servants when once we may have been masters. Fourthly, it will bring the antagonism (or wrath, as was the case here) of our peers, who expect us to act in the same way they do.

How did the Gibeonites manage to overcome such great odds? It was by a substance that they had acquired - faith. By faith the Gibeonites set more store by the might of the LORD God of Israel, than by the might of their neighbours. They correctly weighed up the tales of how Israel came out of Egypt, and came to the conclusion that God was to be feared above anything mankind could do. This building of their faith can be seen in v3, 9-10, 24, as the report of the mighty acts of God for Israel came increasingly near their own door.

And when the inhabitants of Gibeon **heard what Joshua had done unto Jericho and to Ai,** *... And they said unto him, From a very far country thy servants are come because of the name of the LORD thy God: for* **we have heard the fame of him, and all that he did in Egypt,** *And* **all that he did to the two kings of the Amorites, that were beyond Jordan,** *to Sihon king of Heshbon, and to Og king of Bashan, which was at Ashtaroth. ... And they answered Joshua, and said, Because* **it was certainly told thy servants, how that the LORD thy God commanded his servant Moses to give you all the land, and to destroy all the inhabitants of the land from before you,** *therefore we were sore afraid of our lives because of you, and have done this thing. (Jos 9:3, 9-10, 24)*

This is the same for us. By faith we hear reports, but do not see directly what God has reported to us. Our faith is in the testimony of eyewitnesses in the Bible, just as theirs was in the word of eyewitnesses, which tells us that the judgement of the world is coming increasingly near to us. Like the Gibeonites we can choose to capitulate and seek refuge with our judge (v24), or like the nations we can see the same signs, but choose instead to set ourselves against God (v2). Jesus will treat us just as Joshua did, so let's look at the process:

1) Confession of faith in coming judgement (v24)
2) Confession of humility in face of power greater than ours (v24)
3) Giving up, and confession of trust in his mercy (v25)
4) Deliverance (v26)

Food for thought

v18 - Israel had sworn and would not go back on their oath, even though it would have been simple to do so. They had implemented the principles which David later spoke of:

> *In whose eyes a vile person is contemned; but he honoureth them that fear the LORD.* **He that sweareth to his own hurt, and changeth not.** *(Psa 15:4)*

Joshua 10

How the Gibeonites inadvertently helped Joshua conquer the land

Joshua took the cities of the Amorites one after another in quick succession. This was because their men of war had left their cities defenceless in order to fight with Israel at Gilgal:

> *Wherefore Adonizedek king of Jerusalem sent unto Hoham king of Hebron, and unto Piram king of Jarmuth, and unto Japhia king of Lachish, and unto Debir king of Eglon, saying, Come up unto me, and help me, that we may smite Gibeon: for it hath made peace with Joshua and with the children of Israel. Therefore the five kings of the Amorites, the king of Jerusalem, the king of Hebron, the king of Jarmuth, the king of Lachish, the king of Eglon, gathered themselves together, and went up, they and all their hosts, and encamped before Gibeon, and made war against it. (Jos 10:3-5)*

They had then been mostly struck down as they fled. This was why Joshua felt it so important to pursue these soldiers and strike them before they reached their fortified cities, and why he took the unusual step of asking God to extend the daylight. If they reached their cities then those cities would have been defended and difficult to take:

> *Then spake Joshua to the LORD in the day when the LORD delivered up the Amorites before the children of Israel, and he said in the sight of Israel, Sun, stand thou still upon Gibeon; and thou, Moon, in the valley of Ajalon. And the sun stood still, and the moon stayed, until the people had avenged themselves upon their enemies. Is not this written in the book of Jasher? So the sun stood still in the midst of heaven, and hasted not to go down about a whole day. And there was no day like that before it or after it, that the LORD hearkened unto the voice of a man: for the LORD fought for Israel. (Jos 10:12-14)*

We can see from chapter 9 verses 1-2 that the call had already gone out to the five other nations to gather armies against Israel. So Joshua had a short length of time to fight with the Amorites before these all came down to join the battle, and he would be attacked from all sides. Because of his quick victory, Israel was prepared for these armies as they came down, numbering "as the sand that is on the seashore in multitude":

> *And it came to pass, when Jabin king of Hazor had heard those things, that he sent to Jobab king of Madon, and to the king of Shimron, and to the king of Achshaph, And to the kings that were on the north of the mountains, and of the plains south of Chinneroth, and in the valley, and in the borders of Dor on the west, And to the Canaanite on the east and on the west, and to the Amorite, and the Hittite, and the Perizzite, and the Jebusite in the mountains, and to the Hivite under Hermon in the land of Mizpeh. And they went out, they and all their hosts with them, much people, even as the sand that is upon the sea shore in multitude, with horses and*

chariots very many. And when all these kings were met together, they came and pitched together at the waters of Merom, to fight against Israel. (Jos 11:1-5)

Food for thought

v1 - We tend to think of Jerusalem as a major city. Indeed it had a long history - right back to the time of Abraham - but the king of Jerusalem is afraid. Ai is only a few miles down the hill into the Jordan valley. News would travel fast. His guards on the hill tops to the East of Jerusalem could even have seen the smoke.

v3,5 - The reason why those five kings were confederate together was that they were all Amorites.

Joshua 11

Would you live as a dog or die as a lion?

There was not a city that made peace with the children of Israel, save the Hivites the inhabitants of Gibeon: all other they took in battle. For it was of the LORD to harden their hearts, that they should come against Israel in battle, that he might destroy them utterly, and that they might have no favour, but that he might destroy them, as the LORD commanded Moses. (Jos 11:19-20)

I t looks like these people chose their own fate by refusing to be ruled over by Israel. This passage is referring back to the commandment God gave Moses:

*When thou comest nigh unto a city to fight against it, then **proclaim peace unto it**. And it shall be, if it make thee answer of peace, and open unto thee, then it shall be, that all the people that is found therein shall be tributaries unto thee, and they shall serve thee. And if it will make no peace with thee, but will make war against thee, then thou shalt besiege it: And when the LORD thy God hath delivered it into thine hands, thou shalt smite every male thereof with the edge of the sword: (Deu 20:10-13)*

The spiritual situation is actually the same with us. The name "Joshua" is the same as "Jesus" in Hebrew. Do we make peace with Jesus and serve him, or do we harden our hearts and force him to judge us?

This point is made in Luke, speaking of a king with a great army. Imagine Jesus as the king with the bigger army, and you with the smaller one:

> *Or what king, going to make war against another king, sitteth not down first, and consulteth whether he be able with ten thousand to meet him that cometh against him with twenty thousand? Or else, while the other is yet a great way off, he sendeth an ambassage, and* **desireth conditions of peace.** *So likewise, whosoever he be of you that forsaketh not all that he hath, he cannot be my disciple.* (Luk 14:31-33)

Food for thought

v4 - "Sand which is upon the sea shore" echoes what God had promised to Abraham in Genesis 22:17. Israel were going to grow and the Canaanites were going to diminish. The very success of Israel in taking the land was to be an evidence that God would keep His promise with Abraham. Sadly Israel did not see the relevance of the promises and so failed.

v6 - We might have thought that Israel would have benefited from taking the spoils of war and the weaponry of their enemies. It would have provided them with much needed armaments. Having spent 40 years in the wilderness they would be a poorly equipped army. The destruction of the chariots and rendering of the horses useless for battle may have been to force Israel to realise that deliverance came from God, not from the might of their army.

Joshua 12

Little kings and BIG kings

When you consider all these kings in verses 9 to 24 and the place names where they were king, it's clear that these were very small kingdoms. By virtue of the pace of travel, and perhaps the geography of the land, one king didn't rule over more than he could manage.

It's amazing, then, that we read of the vast areas Sihon and Og ruled on the other side of the Jordan, and when we look on a map we see that these areas were mountainous.

We have a clue as to how this could be:

And the coast of Og king of Bashan, which was of the remnant of the giants, that dwelt at Ashtaroth and at Edrei, (Jos 12:4)

Og was gigantic in stature, so much so that he is described in another place as the last of the true giants:

For only Og king of Bashan remained of the remnant of giants; behold, his bedstead was a bedstead of iron; is it not in Rabbath of the children of Ammon? nine cubits was the length thereof, and four cubits the breadth of it, after the cubit of a man. (Deu 3:11)

This man, so tall and so broad that he needed a specially made iron bed to hold his weight, was someone who appears to have been easily able to cover great distances and enforce his rule with barely a problem.

What do you think this tells us about the time of Noah, when there were many such giants in existence?

Food for thought

Note - This chapter, at the end of the military campaign described in the first eleven chapters, summarises the conquest of the land. Verses 1-6 summarise the work under Moses on the East of Jordan. Verses 7-24 focus on the work of Joshua in the land of Canaan.

v3 - Just a little point about Biblical language. The Dead Sea is called "the Salt Sea". That body of water is never called the Dead Sea in Scripture.

Joshua 13

It's fine for us, but can it become a snare to our children?

Verse 13 tells us that the Geshurites and Maachathites "dwell with Israel to this day",

> *Nevertheless the children of Israel expelled not the Geshurites, nor the Maachathites: but the Geshurites and the Maachathites dwell among the Israelites until this day.* (Jos 13:13)

This is mentioned again in King David's time:

> *And David and his men went up, and invaded the **Geshurites**, and the Gezrites, and the Amalekites: for **those nations were of old the inhabitants of the land**, as thou goest to Shur, even unto the land of Egypt.* (1Sa 27:8)

Notice that the Geshurites are mentioned by name, but not the Maachathites. So had they died out or left the country? I don't think so, because at the same time in history, David marries a wife called Maachah, and look who her father is:

38

Now these were the sons of David, which were born unto him in
Hebron; the firstborn Amnon, of Ahinoam the Jezreelitess; the
*second Daniel, of Abigail the Carmelitess: The third, **Absalom the***
***son of Maachah the daughter of Talmai king of Geshur:** the*
fourth, Adonijah the son of Haggith: (1Ch 3:1-2)

So Maachah was the daughter of the King of Geshur, in other words
the King of the Geshurites. Is this perhaps a clue that the Geshurites
and the Maachathites were one and the same people, or at least by the
time of David were indistinct?

In any case, the point of the scripture mentioning these people is
that Israel should have expelled them at the beginning but didn't, and
the problem with that is that God said the people of the land would
eventually become a snare to the people of Israel:

Take heed to thyself, lest thou make a covenant with the inhabitants
of the land whither thou goest, lest it be for a snare in the midst of
thee: ... And thou take of their daughters unto thy sons, and their
daughters go a whoring after their gods, and make thy sons go a
whoring after their gods. (Exo 34:12, 16)

This is something David should have heeded, rather than taking the
princess of Geshur as his wife.

The question is, did this prophecy come true? Well, Absalom the son
of Maachah certainly didn't do David any good. But the idolatry at least
didn't come in David's time. The idolatry came with another Maachah -
daughter of Absalom and mother of King Asa:

And Rehoboam loved Maachah the daughter of Absalom above
all his wives and his concubines: (for he took eighteen wives,
and threescore concubines; and begat twenty and eight sons, and

threescore daughters.) (2Ch 11:21)

And also concerning Maachah the mother of Asa the king, he removed her from being queen, because she had made an idol in a grove: and Asa cut down her idol, and stamped it, and burnt it at the brook Kidron. (2Ch 15:16)

What do you think are the lessons for us when considering the end result here, and Israel's initial failure to act on a problem that didn't seem that pressing to them at the time?

Food for thought

v13 - The indication here is that Israel were happy with the compromised environment that they dwelt in, which matches exactly the situation in the book of Judges where we are repeatedly advised that the inhabitants of the land dwelt among them, for example Judges 1:29

v22 - The death of Balaam actually took place when Moses was still alive (Numbers 31:1-8) demonstrating that the summaries contained in Joshua sometimes extend back to before the time of Joshua's leadership.

Joshua 14

The LORD is with us: fear them not

In verse 10 Caleb says "the LORD has kept me alive". We don't often think about this aspect of the wilderness journey.

And now, behold, the LORD hath kept me alive, as he said, these forty and five years, even since the LORD spake this word unto Moses, while the children of Israel wandered in the wilderness: and now, lo, I am this day fourscore and five years old. (Jos 14:10)

Israel's destruction in the wilderness is used as an example for our learning in the new testament, so we tend to be familiar with it. But just as God worked for forty years to destroy a whole generation, so He worked to keep Joshua and Caleb alive. This care continued afterwards too, during the dangerous wars they fought with the inhabitants of the land. So their faith in God's ability to save was justified. Here is what they had said generations earlier:

And Joshua the son of Nun, and Caleb the son of Jephunneh, which were of them that searched the land, rent their clothes: And they spake unto all the company of the children of Israel, saying, The *land, which we passed through to search it, is an exceeding good land. If the LORD delight in us, then **he will bring us into this land, and give it us;** a land which floweth with milk and honey. Only rebel not ye against the LORD, **neither fear ye the people of the land;** for they are bread for us: their defence is departed from them, and **the LORD is with us: fear them not.** (Num 14:6-9)*

Having faith that God is bigger than giants

The descendants of Anak, the giants, had been there when the spies looked over the land of promise, and it was these giants that made them afraid to enter it.

And they ascended by the south, and came unto Hebron; where Ahiman, Sheshai, and Talmai, the children of Anak, were. (Now Hebron was built seven years before Zoan in Egypt.) ... But the men that went up with him said, We be not able to go up against the people; for they are stronger than we. And they brought up an evil report of the land which they had searched unto the children of Israel, saying, The land, through which we have gone to search it, is a land that eateth up the inhabitants thereof; and all the people that we saw in it are men of a great stature. And there we saw the giants, the sons of Anak, which come of the giants: and we were in our own sight as grasshoppers, and so we were in their sight. (Num 13:22, 31-33)

Joshua and Caleb were the only ones with the faith that God was bigger than the giants, as noted in the previous section. And this wasn't just an empty faith. They proved their faith in actions by personally driving the Anakim out, relying on the strength of the LORD:

And at that time came Joshua, and cut off the Anakims from the mountains, from Hebron, from Debir, from Anab, and from all the mountains of Judah, and from all the mountains of Israel: Joshua destroyed them utterly with their cities. There was none of the Anakims left in the land of the children of Israel: only in Gaza, in Gath, and in Ashdod, there remained. (Jos 11:21-22)

And unto Caleb the son of Jephunneh he gave a part among the children of Judah, according to the commandment of the LORD to Joshua, even the city of Arba the father of Anak, which city is Hebron. And Caleb drove thence the three sons of Anak, Sheshai, and Ahiman, and Talmai, the children of Anak. (Jos 15:13-14)

Does our own faith in God find its outworking in the things we do? It may not be acts of good works that prove the existence of our faith. It may more likely be the quiet confidence we have in God's plan for us. Joshua and Caleb had that quiet confidence for forty years while they waited for their opportunity to fight the battles they had claimed as young men that they were confident to fight.

Food for thought

v9 - Whilst Joshua is reminding the people what Moses had said as recorded in Numbers 14:22, the language actually echoes what God said to Abraham in Genesis 13:17-18, confirming that the land was being given to them because of what God had said to Abraham.

v10 - The simple mention of 'forty five years' by Caleb provides a valuable time marker. Israel wandered in the wilderness for thirty eight years, so doing the sum: 45 - 38 = 7, we now know that by this time in the book of Joshua Israel have been in the land for seven years.

Joshua 15

Once upon a time there were three giants...

The three giant grandsons of Arba were Sheshai, Ahiman and Talmai, and they were the specific reason Israel failed to enter the promised land. This can be seen by these verses (Num 13:22, 28-33, Deut 1:28, Josh 14:12). Caleb had been one of the twelve spies who personally saw these three giants in Hebron:

> *So they went up, and searched the land from the wilderness of Zin unto Rehob, as men come to Hamath. And they ascended by the south, **and came unto Hebron; where Ahiman, Sheshai, and Talmai, the children of Anak, were**. (Num 13:21-22)*

Caleb's faith allowed him to personally stand up against them when he finally entered the land 40 years later, and possess their city.

> *And unto Caleb the son of Jephunneh he gave a part among the children of Judah, according to the commandment of the LORD to Joshua, even the city of Arba the father of Anak, which city is Hebron. And Caleb drove thence the three sons of Anak, Sheshai, and Ahiman, and Talmai, the children of Anak. (Jos 15:13-14)*

This area is still called Hebron today, which is now in the West Bank administered by the Palestinian Authority. Looking on a map we can see that rather than the city name being changed to the historical Hebron, Kirjath Arba (the city of Arba) now exists alongside Hebron. The giant's name lives on!

It is amazing that this is the case, and that people exist today who wish to bring back the name of this father of the giants who resisted Israel's claim to the land. More amazingly still, it appears to be the Jews themselves who established the town and brought back the name. This is possibly because way back in history Abraham, Isaac and Jacob all lived peacefully in Kirjath Arba. I wonder if the giant was there even then?

> *And Sarah died in **Kirjatharba; the same is Hebron** in the land of Canaan: and Abraham came to mourn for Sarah, and to weep for her. (Gen 23:2)*

> *And Jacob came unto Isaac his father unto Mamre, unto **the city of Arbah, which is Hebron**, where Abraham and Isaac sojourned. (Gen 35:27)*

Food for thought

v4 - The mention of "Azmon" and the border shows how very precisely the instructions in Numbers 34:4-5 were being followed.

v15 - In mentioning both the current and old name of the city, those who would later read the record are given enough information to be able to link the city with previous events.

Joshua 16

Ignoring one small verse of scripture brings generations of repercussions

And they drave not out the Canaanites that dwelt in Gezer: but the Canaanites dwell among the Ephraimites unto this day, and serve under tribute. (Jos 16:10)

The Canaanites living at Gezer should have been driven out according to the commandment of God, but were still around even at the time of Solomon. And even then, when the kingdom of Israel was at its height, Solomon couldn't finish the job himself. He somehow persuaded Pharaoh to come and do it for him:

For Pharaoh king of Egypt had gone up, and taken Gezer, and burnt it with fire, and slain the Canaanites that dwelt in the city, and given it for a present unto his daughter, Solomon's wife. (1Ki 9:16)

Pharaoh did this as a gift to his daughter who had married Solomon. There is something fundamentally wrong with what went on here, and yet these momentous things are hidden in just a few verses. We have to read between the lines and gather information from here and there to piece it together.

God had said clearly and without any ambiguity that he wanted the Canaanites destroyed:

*When the LORD thy God shall bring thee into the land whither thou goest to possess it, and hath cast out many nations before thee, the Hittites, and the Girgashites, and the Amorites, and **the Canaanites**, and the Perizzites, and the Hivites, and the Jebusites, seven nations greater and mightier than thou; And when the LORD thy God shall deliver them before thee; **thou shalt smite them, and utterly destroy them; thou shalt make no covenant with them, nor shew mercy unto them: Neither shalt thou make marriages with them;** thy daughter thou shalt not give unto his son, nor his daughter shalt thou take unto thy son. (Deu 7:1-3)*

We saw in verse 10 that this hadn't been done. God also said quite clearly that Israel were not to go back to Egypt in any way: specifically kings were not to go there for horses:

*Thou shalt in any wise set him king over thee, whom the LORD thy God shall choose: one from among thy brethren shalt thou set king over thee... **But he shall not multiply horses to himself, nor cause the people to return to Egypt**, to the end that he should multiply horses: forasmuch as the LORD hath said unto you, Ye shall henceforth return no more that way. **Neither shall he multiply wives to himself,** that his heart turn not away: neither shall he greatly multiply to himself silver and gold. (Deu 17:15-17)*

So we know that what went on here was a big deal to God. Israel and

Solomon were diverging in a major way from God's wishes. In fact, all these disobeyed laws coincide and come to a head at Gezer. Solomon's marriage, paid for by Pharaoh's invasion of Gezer, was a diplomatic union between Egypt and Israel in order that horses and chariots might be bought from Egypt and sold at a profit by Solomon:

> *And Solomon had horses brought out of Egypt, and linen yarn: the king's merchants received the linen yarn at a price. And a chariot came up and went out of Egypt for six hundred shekels of silver, and an horse for an hundred and fifty: and so for all the kings of the Hittites, and for the kings of Syria, did they bring them out by their means. (1Ki 10:28-29)*

We know that this related to Gezer because Gezer became a storage city for these goods.

> *And Solomon built **Gezer**, and Bethhoron the nether, And Baalath, and Tadmor in the wilderness, in the land, And all the cities of store that Solomon had, and **cities for his chariots, and cities for his horsemen**, and that which Solomon desired to build in Jerusalem, and in Lebanon, and in all the land of his dominion. (1Ki 9:17-19)*

The price that Israel paid for ignoring God's seemingly insignificant commandments was annihilation, since this union with Egypt started off the path Solomon took to rejecting God and adopting idols, which ultimately degenerated to the whole nation's rejection of the true God. How often do we ignore a seemingly small part of God's will, thinking it doesn't matter?

Food for thought

v4 - It is only said of the children of Joseph that "they took their inheritance", implying that all the other tribes were compromised in some way.

v10 - The idea of serving under tribute became a feature of the compromised settlement in the land in the days of the Judges. For example Judges 1:28,30,33,35.

Joshua 17

Can jealousy take generations to surface?

*But Zelophehad, the son of Hepher, the son of Gilead, the son of Machir, the son of Manasseh, had no sons, but daughters: and these are the names of his daughters, **Mahlah, and Noah, Hoglah, Milcah, and Tirzah**. And they came near before Eleazar the priest, and before Joshua the son of Nun, and before the princes, saying, The LORD commanded Moses to give us an inheritance among our brethren. Therefore according to the commandment of the LORD he gave them an inheritance among the brethren of their father. **And there fell ten portions to Manasseh, beside the land of Gilead and Bashan, which were on the other side Jordan; Because the daughters of Manasseh had an inheritance among his sons**: and the rest of Manasseh's sons had the land of Gilead. (Jos 17:3-6)*

The daughters of Zelophehad are lesser known Bible characters, although they appear relatively often, in Numbers 26:33, 27:1-11, 36:1-13, and 1Chron 7:15, as well as in this chapter. Theirs was an important test case for the way the law of Moses would be applied in cases where a man had only daughters and was in danger of losing his family inheritance. This appears to have been the last case Moses dealt with before his death, or at least it is recorded last, which shows how important it was.

The repercussions of giving inheritance to daughters instead of just sons may have been massive, because the Bible hints it may have led to the strife between Ephraim and Manasseh in Judges 12, where 42,000 Ephraimites died.

Then Jephthah gathered together all the men of Gilead, and fought with Ephraim: and the men of Gilead smote Ephraim, because **they said, Ye Gileadites are fugitives of Ephraim among the Ephraimites, and among the Manassites.** *(Jdg 12:4)*

Is it possible that these Gileadites were the offspring of Zelophehad's daughters? If so, could this strife have been a result of the tribe of Ephraim's jealousy that the tribe of Manasseh got more land than they did? Is this related to their complaint in verse 18?

Food for thought

v4 - Notice that disputes were dealt with by Joshua *and* Eleazar. Eleazar was the priest, the son of Aaron. It was God's land they were quarrelling over, and therefore His representative – Eleazar – worked with his military leader, Joshua, to resolve it.

v14 - In complaining about being given 'but one lot', Joseph is actually complaining about God's generosity. The land was not his to have, it was a gift from God - so he should have been happy to accept what God offered. How about ourselves?

v18 - "though they have chariots of iron" would not be a problem to men of faith. This is the point that Joshua is making.

Joshua 18

Big brothers protecting their little brother

Benjamin was the little brother of Joseph, son of the same mother:

> The sons of Rachel Jacob's wife; Joseph, and Benjamin.
(Gen 46:19)

He was also the boy that Judah, his half brother, pledged his life to protect:

> And Judah said unto Israel his father, Send the lad with me, and we will arise and go; that we may live, and not die, both we, and thou, and also our little ones. **I will be surety for him**; of my hand shalt thou require him: if I bring him not unto thee, and set him before thee, then let me bear the blame for ever: (Gen 43:8-9)

Now generations later, all three have grown into large families, part of the 12 tribes of Israel. So isn't it lovely that when we see the land of Israel divided up between these tribes, that Benjamin is nestled safely between Joseph and Judah?

53

And the lot of the tribe of the children of Benjamin came up according to their families: and the coast of their lot came forth **between the children of Judah and the children of Joseph.** *(Jos 18:11)*

Food for thought

v7 - The Levites had a job to do. They were to minister to the people and present their sacrifices to God. That privileged role was their inheritance - not land. Do we think of our ability to serve God as an inheritance more valuable than material things?

v11 - Notice that Benjamin is the first in the list of those for whom the lot was cast. So even though Benjamin was the last born son of Jacob he is the first to be told his inheritance.

Joshua 19

Zorah and Eshtaol

And the seventh lot came out for the tribe of the children of Dan according to their families. And the coast of their inheritance was Zorah, and Eshtaol, and Irshemesh, (Jos 19:40-41)

In-between Zorah and Eshtaol is the place where the tribe of Dan camped, and this is the same place where the Spirit of the Lord began to move Samson to do the work He had intended for him:

*And the Spirit of the LORD began to move him at times in the camp of Dan **between Zorah and Eshtaol**. (Jdg 13:25)*

It means that the tribe of Dan hadn't yet taken their inheritance at the time of Samson, and had remained living in tents all that time.

Also it means that it was the Philistines that prevented them from taking their land. Samson's mission is greatly clarified by this discovery – namely that his fight against the Philistines was in order that his countrymen (the tribe of Dan) might take their inheritance. Had Samson not fallen foul of Delilah, he may have completed his mission. But instead the tribe of Dan eventually give up and move away from the area to find a new place to live:

> *In those days there was no king in Israel: and in those days the tribe of the Danites sought them an inheritance to dwell in; for unto that day all their inheritance had not fallen unto them among the tribes of Israel. ... And there went from thence of the family of the Danites, **out of Zorah and out of Eshtaol**, six hundred men appointed with weapons of war. ... and came unto Laish, unto a people that were at quiet and secure: and they smote them with the edge of the sword, and burnt the city with fire ... And they built a city, and dwelt therein. And they called the name of the city Dan, after the name of Dan their father, who was born unto Israel: howbeit the name of the city was Laish at the first. (Jdg 18:1, 11, 27-29)*

Food for thought

v1 - The distribution of the land was determined by God. Because of Simeon's sin (see Genesis 34:25-31), his tribe's allocation was to be within the territory of Judah. This was a direct fulfilment of the prophecy uttered by Jacob at the end of his life. God would "divide in Jacob and scattered in Israel" (Genesis 49:5-7).

v13 - Gittah-Hepher is the same place as Gath-Hepher, seen in 2 Kings 14:25. So we might conclude that Jonah was from the tribe of Zebulon.

Joshua 20

Caleb's dwindling inheritance

C an you imagine the following conversation:

"Caleb, I promise you can have all the land you walked on when you spied out the promised land" (*Numbers 14:24, Deuteronomy 1:35-36*).

"But you'll have to wait 40 years for it" (*Joshua 14:6-10*).

"Actually, when I said 'all the land' I meant just one city for now, and its suburbs" (*Joshua 14:13-14*).

(40 years later).

"You can go and live in it now. But you'll have to fight three giants for it first" (*Joshua 15:13-14, and see Numbers 13:22, 32-33*).

"By the way, now you've fought the giants for it; I'm allocating your city to anyone who's fleeing the law because they've committed manslaughter. Hope you don't mind. So it'll be a bit more crowded than you first thought" *(Joshua 20:1-7).*

"Oh, and didn't I mention? There's a whole bunch of Levites I've just promised the actual city to. And its surrounding land. So is it ok if you and your family move out and just have the villages?" *(Joshua 21:11-12).*

How would you feel if that were you?

> *And what shall I more say? for the time would fail me to tell of Gedeon, and of Barak, and of Samson, and of Jephthae; of David also, and Samuel, and of the prophets:* **Who through faith subdued kingdoms,** *wrought righteousness, obtained promises, stopped the mouths of lions, ... And* **these all, having obtained a good report through faith, received not the promise:** *(Heb 11:32-33, 39)*

Caleb seems to get a mention here in Hebrews 11, even though he isn't named. He was the one who, with Joshua, and by God's help, subdued the land of Canaan. Like Abraham he had to wait to inherit the promised land. He had the faith to realise all things are temporary in this world and not worth having compared to eternal promises. Just as Abraham was promised the land of Israel but didn't live long enough to occupy it, so Caleb and his family still wait for the resurrection where all God's promises will be delivered in full.

Food for thought

v1-6 - The appointment of the cities of refuge shows that the LORD was merciful to those who may have erred dreadfully but were not premeditated murderers. This foreshadows the work of the Lord Jesus Christ. Of the faithful servants of God who are baptised into Jesus it is said that they have "fled for refuge" (Hebrews 6:18)

v9 - The cities of refuge were for the benefit of both Jew and Gentile (the stranger) so here we see another aspect of the provision of God in Christ, who died to save both the Jew and the Gentile.

Joshua 21

Caleb's heir

In the previous chapter we looked at God's promises to Caleb, and the fact that he didn't inherit the land in his own lifetime. Here is the promise of God to Caleb:

> *And the LORD ... sware, saying, Surely there shall not one of these men of this evil generation see that good land, which I sware to give unto your fathers, Save Caleb the son of Jephunneh; he shall see it, and **to him will I give the land that he hath trodden upon, and to his children**, because he hath wholly followed the LORD.* (Deu 1:34-36)

Caleb had specifically been to Hebron, because it was there that he and the other spies had seen the giants, the sons of Anak. But when we come to this chapter in Joshua, the city is given away to the Levites:

> *Which the children of Aaron, being of the families of the Kohathites, who were of the children of Levi, had: for theirs was the first lot. And they gave them the city of Arba the father of Anak, which city is Hebron, in the hill country of Judah, with the suburbs thereof*

round about it. But the fields of the city, and the villages thereof, gave they to Caleb the son of Jephunneh for his possession. (Jos 21:10-12)

But we know that God always keeps His word, so how do we understand the contradiction?

As we saw in the previous chapter, God will keep His promises to Caleb and to others listed in Hebrews 11, because He will raise them up from the dead.

And I think there's also something else. I think Caleb's descendants may have inherited Hebron after all. Take a look at who reigned over Judah from that city:

And the time that David was king in Hebron over the house of Judah was seven years and six months. (2Sa 2:11)

Now Caleb had been a leader of Judah:

*And Moses by the commandment of the LORD sent them from the wilderness of Paran: all those men were **heads of the children of Israel.** ... **Of the tribe of Judah, Caleb** the son of Jephunneh. (Num 13:3, 6)*

And one of his wives was Ephrath:

And when Azubah was dead, Caleb took unto him Ephrath, which bare him Hur. (1Ch 2:19)

And guess who descended from Ephrath?

Now David was the son of that Ephrathite of Bethlehemju-

dah, whose name was Jesse; and he had eight sons: and the man went among men for an old man in the days of Saul. (1Sa 17:12)

So, if David descended from Caleb, then it was through David that the promises of God to Caleb were fulfilled. It was also by being Caleb's descendant that David could claim to be a legitimate heir to the throne, because God had promised the land of Israel to Caleb.

Food for thought

v11 - In describing Hebron as a city "in the hill country of Judea" we are provided with an indication of the home of Elizabeth and Zacharias (Luke 1:39) for this is how the place where they lived is described in the gospel. It is a small example of how the Old and New Testament text compliment and illuminate one another if we read the text carefully.

v43 - The oath that God had made to give the land, had been made to Abraham:

> *For all the land which thou seest, to thee will I give it, and to thy seed for ever.* (Gen 13:15)

So this point marks a fulfilment, in part, of the promises to Abraham.

Joshua 22

Assuming the worst intentions

The fighting men of the tribes of Reuben, Gad, and Manasseh had shown themselves to be faithful, dedicated, and zealous men. For a long time they had been without their families in order that they might keep their promise of fighting alongside the other tribes in displacing the people of Canaan.

When the work was finally done, it wasn't they that came to Joshua, eagerly requesting that they be allowed to finish the work and go home to their families, but it was Joshua who came to them. This suggests that they were fully dedicated to continuing the work until it was completely done.

Having thus proven their dedication to God, and returning home, they set up an altar of witness... and incurred the wrath of the rest of Israel. Israel had assumed, wrongly, that they were defying the Lord and going against His commandments. Wouldn't you think that they would have trusted their brothers a little more than that, especially given their faithful track record? Wouldn't you think that they would have gone to their brothers and meekly enquired what they were doing rather than accusing them, and gathering all of Israel to war against them?

And when the children of Israel heard of it, the whole congregation
of the children of Israel gathered themselves together at Shiloh, to
go up to war against them. (Jos 22:12)

When we see a fellow believer, or even a group of believers, doing
something we assume is against God's word; shouldn't we first go and
obtain the facts before jumping to conclusions? Is it not worth looking at
the "track record" of a party before assuming they are guilty? Sometimes
our brother may do something which, though out of the ordinary, is
still a justifiable act of worship, and until we ask them personally about
it, we should assume that they are innocent until proven guilty, and not
the other way round. If we are in doubt about this principle, then we
have only to look at the way Jesus was treated by those around him.
They often assumed he was doing wrong, but that was only because
they didn't understand the ways of God as well as he did.

Sharing the spoil

Many of the Reubenites, Gadites and Manassites had stayed behind to
look after the livestock and children. This must have included many
men, possibly even some who were trained for war. The temptation
would have been there for the men who "did all the work" of conquering
the land to keep all the spoil to themselves and not give any to those who
stayed behind. Hence Joshua's specific command in verse 8 to share it
with those who had stayed behind. These were not wages, but extras
that God had given them:

And he spake unto them, saying, Return with much riches unto
your tents, and with very much cattle, with silver, and with gold,
and with brass, and with iron, and with very much raiment: **divide**
the spoil of your enemies with your brethren. *(Jos 22:8)*

The point is that God was giving them the land and had divided it up among the people. So it was only right that they did the same and divided up the spoils they had taken in war. These spoils were extra: over and above what God had promised them. I wonder if the same principle applies to us too? I know of many wonderful examples of believers who share the extras that God has given them, for example those with large homes who constantly have others over to stay, those who are excellent cooks and have sufficient means to provide for groups of young people to enjoy a good meal and have fellowship together. Others have time on their hands and use it well to go and visit the elderly or those with great voices who go to sing to them. These are all extras, and I suspect that the ones who share their extras are in turn enriched themselves.

Food for thought

v11-12 - The Proverb counsels:

> *He that answereth a matter before he heareth it, it is folly and shame unto him. (Pro 18:13)*

A wise counsel which should have been understood and implemented by the whole nation at this time. We can easily fall into the same way of thinking. We may listen to one person speaking of another and simply assume that the one speaking is presenting a complete picture. Wrong judgement can flow from someone who has no intention of misrepresenting another. The error is simply a matter of not being in possession of all the facts.

Joshua 23

Do only the good bits of the Bible apply to you?

J oshua makes a very valid point in verses 14-15. Everything good that God promised to do for you, He has done, so you can be sure that He can also do every bad thing He promised to do to you.

*And, behold, this day I am going the way of all the earth: and ye know in all your hearts and in all your souls, that **not one thing hath failed of all the good things which the LORD your God spake concerning you;** all are come to pass unto you, and not one thing hath failed thereof. Therefore it shall come to pass, that as all good things are come upon you, which the LORD your God promised you; **so shall the LORD bring upon you all evil things,** until he have destroyed you from off this good land which the LORD your God hath given you. (Jos 23:14-15)*

We live in a time far removed from the Old Testament days, yet we still take a lot of lessons of how God works from the Old Testament. Ask yourself: "am I being selective in what I apply to myself from the Old Testament?". We often quote the promises of God which relate to good things, and then relate them to ourselves, such as:

*There shall not any man be able to stand before thee all the days
of thy life: as I was with Moses, so **I will be with thee: I will not
fail thee, nor forsake thee.** (Jos 1:5)*

Should we not also apply the principles of the Old Testament which
relate to His curses, if we behave in a disobedient manner? God deals
with us as His children, just as He did the children of Israel. He was *their*
Father and is *our* Father. If we disobey or turn away, we can be sure
that He will correct us using similar principles as He did with Israel in
order to turn us back to Him. If we turn back to Him wholeheartedly
and serve Him, He may bless us in a similar manner too.

The plea of Joshua to them is the same as for us:

*Take good heed therefore unto yourselves, that ye love the LORD
your God. (Jos 23:11)*

One man shall chase a thousand

Joshua now addresses the problem of the continued invasion of the land
after his death. In verse 10 he quotes the covenant in Leviticus 26:8.
But actually it's a misquote:

***One man of you shall chase a thousand:** for the LORD your
God, he it is that fighteth for you, as he hath promised you. (Jos
23:10)*

Quoted from:

*And **five of you shall chase an hundred**, and an **hundred of
you shall put ten thousand to flight:** and your enemies shall
fall before you by the sword. (Lev 26:8)*

The Leviticus passage promises five will chase a hundred, or a hundred will overcome ten thousand. So why has Joshua inflated the figure? Maybe he's taken the figure from another promise:

> *How should one chase a thousand, and two put ten thousand to flight, except their Rock had sold them, and the LORD had shut them up?* (Deu 32:30)

This is the correct figure, one chasing a thousand, but actually this is their enemies chasing them, not them chasing their enemies. Joshua has turned it around. This is apt because God is here saying that He will work against them if they disobeyed, in the same way as He would be for them if they obeyed. This is what Joshua goes on to talk about in the next verses (11-13).

This promise was proved true several times by different Israelites. Samson was the one who literary fulfilled it by slaying a thousand:

> *And he found a new jawbone of an ass, and put forth his hand, and took it, and **slew a thousand men** therewith.* (Jdg 15:15)

Also Gideon:

> *And the Midianites and the Amalekites and all the children of the east lay along in the valley **like grasshoppers for multitude; and their camels were without number, as the sand by the sea side for multitude.** ... And they stood every man in his place round about the camp: and all the host ran, and cried, and fled. And **the three hundred blew the trumpets, and the LORD set every man's sword against his fellow, even throughout all the host: and the host fled** to Bethshittah in Zererath, and to the border of Abelmeholah, unto Tabbath.* (Jdg 7:12, 21-22)

And Jonathan, the son of King Saul:

> *And that first slaughter, which Jonathan and his armourbearer made, was about twenty men, within as it were an half acre of land, which a yoke of oxen might plow. And there was trembling in the host, in the field, and among all the people: the garrison, and the spoilers, they also trembled, and the earth quaked: so it was a very great trembling. And the watchmen of Saul in Gibeah of Benjamin looked; and, behold, the multitude melted away, and they went on beating down one another. (1Sa 14:14-16)*

The promise was ultimately completed when the young man, David, put the whole army of the Philistines to flight by himself, while trusting totally in God:

> *Therefore David ran, and stood upon the Philistine, and took his sword, and drew it out of the sheath thereof, and slew him, and cut off his head therewith. And when the Philistines saw their champion was dead, they fled. (1Sa 17:51)*

This promise and these events are a foreshadowing of Jesus, and how he would by himself destroy the power of death for everyone who believes.

Food for thought

v1 - Even though Israel had been "given rest from their enemies" they had not entered into the rest that God had prepared. They had been warned about that in Deuteronomy 12:9 and it is confirmed in Hebrews 4:8 that Joshua never gave them rest. That was the job of his greater namesake, Jesus.

v3 - The old man Joshua had been the leader of the nation for all those years. But he reminded Israel that the land had been taken because of the Lord's involvement. How easy it would have been for him to emphasise his part in the battles. In like manner we can revel in what we have done rather than giving glory to God for the things we have achieved.

Joshua 24

Crossing over the flood: Starting a new life

N otice that in Joshua's command to the people that they put away their idols, he draws on the example of Abraham. Here is his first point about Abraham:

*And Joshua said unto all the people, Thus saith the LORD God of Israel, Your fathers **dwelt on the other side of the flood** in old time, even Terah, the father of Abraham, and the father of Nachor: and **they served other gods**. (Jos 24:2)*

Now compare this with his statement to Israel:

*Now therefore fear the LORD, and serve him in sincerity and in truth: and **put away the gods which your fathers served on the other side of the flood**, and in Egypt; and serve ye the LORD. And if it seem evil unto you to serve the LORD, choose you this day whom ye will serve; whether the gods which your fathers served that were **on the other side of the flood**, or the gods of the Amorites, in whose land ye dwell: but as for me and my house, we will serve the LORD. (Jos 24:14-15)*

So it's clear that with this phrase "on the other side of the flood" he is drawing their attention to Abraham.

Why?

Well, Joshua is saying that Abraham and his family were idolatrous, or were beginning to be so, and that God's urgent action in taking Abraham out of that place was a clean start for him. Abraham from that point on only served the true God.

The point Joshua is making to the Israelites is that they, like Abraham, should take the opportunity of this journey to a new land, to start afresh.

Now it's your turn and my turn to think about our life. Are we serving God only, or have other things contrary to God crept in to our lives? Are these things threatening to take the place of God? If you believe this is the case, then drastic action to start afresh as needed and, as with Abraham and the Israelites, taking a journey to a new place can be the turning point allowing us to leave behind bad influences, corrupting habits, and to place God at the centre of our new life.

Food for thought

v23 - The call to put away the strange gods did not remove idols from the nation because during the time of the Judges (Judges 10:16) the people again needed to put away their idols.

v32 - Are we to presume, because this chapter speaks of the end of Joshua's life (see verse 29), that Joseph's bones were not buried until after Israel had been in the land for quite some time? If so, where were they kept until their burial, and what do you think was the reason for the delay?

Epilogue

Joshua now passes from the scene and hands over the batten of responsibility to the elders who survive him. However, whilst he may not be with them any longer, his incredible legacy lives on in them:

> *And Israel served the LORD all the days of Joshua, and all the days of the elders that overlived Joshua, and which had known all the works of the LORD, that he had done for Israel. (Jos 24:31)*

And so the message of the book is this:

What legacy will you leave?

Other books in the series

The *Food for Thought in the Old Testament* series aims to build up into a library of books covering each chapter of the Old Testament of the Bible. Why not collect them all?

Sign up here for publication announcements and special offers and bundle deals:

www.woodland.press/sign-up

Genesis	Joshua	Ezra, Nehemiah & Esther	Jeremiah & Lamentations
Exodus	Judges & Ruth	Job	Ezekiel
Leviticus	1 & 2 Samuel	Psalms	Daniel & Hosea
Numbers	1 & 2 Kings	Proverbs, Ecclesiastes & Song of Solomon	Joel to Nahum
Deuteronomy	1 & 2 Chronicles	Isaiah	Habakkuk to Malachi

Index

A

Aaron 51, 60
Abelmeholah 68
Abigail 39
Abiram 2
Abraham 8, 25, 33, 35, 43, 45, 58, 62, 71, 72
Absalom 39
Adonijah 39
Adonizedek 28, 31
Ahiman 42-44
Ahinoam 39
Ajalon 32
altar 23, 63
Amalekites 38, 68
Ammon 36
Amnon 39
Amorite 12, 26-29, 31-33, 47, 71
Anab 43
Anak 42-44, 60
Aram 20
Arba 43-45, 60
armourbearer 69
Ashdod 43

Ashtaroth 27, 29, 36
ass 18, 68
Azmon 45
Azubah 61

B

Baalath 48
Balaam 40
baptised 7, 8, 58
Barak 58
Bashan 27, 29, 36, 50
bedstead 36
believe 7, 19, 64, 65, 72
Benjamin 53, 54, 69
besiege 34
Bethel 22, 24, 25
Bethhoron 48
Bethshittah 68
Bible 1, 2, 4, 18, 30, 37, 50, 51, 66, 74, 76
blame 21, 53
bless 2, 5, 67
blood 20
body 23, 37
boldly 13
bones 72
border 10, 32, 45, 68
born 13, 18, 20, 39, 54, 56
bound 19
boy 19, 20, 53
brass 16, 64

bravery 12
breach 19
bread 42
brethren 8, 13, 28, 47, 50, 64
bronze 15
brother 18, 19, 53, 63, 64
build 11, 23, 29, 42, 48, 56, 74
bury 23, 72

C

Caleb 41-44, 57, 58, 60-62
  camels 68
  camp 16, 55, 68
  campaign 37
  Canaan 12, 28, 32, 35, 37, 45-47, 58, 63
  capture 24
  Carmelitess 39
  cattle 64
  champion 69
  chariot 33, 35, 48, 51
  Chinneroth 32
  Christ 20, 58, 59
  circumcise 12, 13
  city 4, 5, 13, 15, 17, 22-25, 28, 31-34, 43-46, 48, 56-62
  coast 28, 36, 54, 55
  coin 27
  commandment 5, 20, 34, 43, 44, 46, 48, 50, 61, 63
  complain 51
  concubines 39
  condemning 5

confederate 27, 33
confession 30
confident 43
congregation 64
conquer 14, 31, 37, 64
conscience 19, 21
covenant 7, 8, 10, 13, 20, 39, 47, 67
crossing 6, 7, 9, 12, 13, 71
cubit 36, 37
curse 16, 67

D

Daniel 17, 39
Danites 56
Dathan 2
daughter 18, 39, 40, 46, 47, 50, 51
David 17, 30, 38, 39, 58, 61, 62, 69
death 1, 4, 15, 16, 40, 51, 67, 69
Debir 28, 31, 43
dedicate 11, 63
defence 13, 31, 32, 42
defiled 23
Delilah 55
deliver 30, 32, 34, 35, 47, 58
descendant 20, 42, 61, 62
destroy 4, 15, 16, 24, 27-29, 34, 35, 41, 43, 47, 66, 69
devote 15-17
disciple 35
disobey 48, 67, 68
disputes 51

dominion 48

E

Ebal 23, 25
    echo 11, 35, 43
    Edrei 36
    Eglon 28, 31
    Egypt 2, 6, 7, 10, 13, 25-27, 29, 38, 42, 46-48, 71
    elders 73
    Eleazar 50, 51
    Elizabeth 62
    encamped 28, 31
    Ephraim 46, 51
    Ephrath 61
    Eshtaol 55, 56
    eyewitnesses 30

F

fail 2, 14, 35, 40, 44, 58, 66, 67
    faint 27
    faith 5, 8, 17, 19, 20, 27, 29, 30, 41-44, 52, 58, 63
    family 5, 16, 25, 29, 51, 53-56, 58, 60, 63, 72
    father 3, 8, 10, 38, 43-45, 50, 53, 56, 60, 67, 71
    fearful 20
    fellowship 65
    firstborn 39
    flood 71, 72
    folly 65
    foreskins 12

fugitives 51
fulfill 56, 62, 68

G

Gad 11, 63, 64
garrison 69
gate 13, 23
Gath 43
Gath-Hepher 56
Gaza 43
generosity 51
Gentile 27, 59
Gerizim 25
Geshur 38, 39
Gezer 38, 46, 48
giant 36, 37, 42, 44, 45, 57, 60
Gibeah 69
Gibeon 26-32, 34
Gideon 58, 68
gigantic 36
Gilead 50, 51
Gilgal 10, 11, 31
Girgashites 47
Gittah-Hepher 56
gold 15-18, 47, 64
grandsons 44
grasshoppers 42, 68
guilty 64

H

Haggith 39
    Hamath 44
    Hamor 13
    hanged 23
    harlot 4, 15
    Hazor 32
    heap 9, 23
    hearkened 2, 13, 32
    heart 6, 12, 19, 27, 34, 35, 47, 66
    heaven 27, 32
    Hebrews 5, 19, 58, 59, 61, 69
    Hebron 28, 31, 39, 42-45, 60-62
    Hepher 50
    Hermon 32
    Heshbon 27, 29
    hewn 23
    Hittite 28, 32, 47, 48
    Hivite 28, 32, 34, 47
    Hoglah 50
    Hoham 28, 31
    honey 10, 42
    horse 32, 35, 47, 48
    horsemen 48
    Hoshea 3
    house 4, 15, 24, 61, 71
    husband 5, 20

I

idol 39, 40, 48, 71, 72
    influences 72

Isaac 45

J

Jabin 32
Jacob 13, 20, 45, 53, 54, 56
Japhia 28, 31
Jarmuth 28, 31
Jasher 32
jawbone 68
jealousy 50, 51
Jebusite 28, 32, 47
Jephthah 51, 58
Jephunneh 41, 43, 44, 60, 61
Jericho 4, 5, 11, 15-17, 25, 28, 29
Jerusalem 28, 31, 33, 48
Jesse 62
Jesus 2, 5, 17, 20, 26, 27, 30, 35, 58, 64, 69
Jew 45, 59
Jezreelitess 39
Jobab 32
Jonathan 69
Jordan 1, 6, 7, 9-13, 26-29, 33, 36, 37, 50
Joseph 20, 24, 49, 51, 53, 54, 72
Judah 43, 44, 53, 54, 56, 60, 61
Judas 20
Judea 62
judge 20, 30, 35, 65
Judges 24, 40, 49, 51, 72

K

Kidron 40

   kingdom 3, 17, 36, 46, 58

   Kirjatharba 45

   knives 12

   Kohathites 60

   Korah 2

L

Lachish 28, 31

   Laish 56

   laws 48

   lead 1, 2, 7, 16, 22, 40, 51, 61, 70

   Lebanon 28, 48

   legacy 73

   Levi 13, 60

   Levites 54, 58, 60

   lion 34, 58

   livestock 64

   lodged 22, 25

   love 20, 39, 53, 67

   loyalty 2

   Luke 27, 35, 62

M

Maachah 38-40

   Machir 50

   Madon 32

   magnified 7

   Mahlah 50

Mamre 45

Manasseh 11, 50, 51, 63, 64

manslaughter 57

marching 17

marriage 38, 46-48

Mary 20

masters 29

meek 2, 63

melted 12, 69

memorial 10

merchandise 16

merchants 48

mercy 20, 25, 29, 30, 47, 58

Merom 33

messengers 4, 15

metal 16, 17

Midianites 68

midwife 19

Milcah 50

milk 10, 42

miracle 6, 7, 12

Mizpeh 32

moon 32

Moses 1, 2, 7, 8, 11, 17, 20, 23, 27, 29, 34, 37, 40, 41, 43, 50, 51, 61, 67

murderers 58

N

neighbours 28, 29

Noah 37, 50

number 9, 11, 18, 32, 68

Nun 1, 2, 41, 50

O

oath 30, 62
  obey 7, 20, 68
  offering 15, 23
  Oshea 3
  oxen 18, 69

P

Palestinian 45
  parable 26, 27
  Paran 61
  perdition 19
  Perez 19, 20
  Perizzite 28, 32, 47
  Pharaoh 2, 6, 46, 48
  Pharez 19, 20
  Pharisees 5
  Philistine 55, 69
  plains 11, 32
  portions 50
  possess 15, 25, 44, 47, 61, 65
  power 30, 69
  precious metals 16
  premeditated 58
  prepare 9-11, 32, 69
  pride 29
  priest 7, 50, 51

princes 50
princess 39
promises 27, 35, 58, 60-62, 66, 68
prophecy 39, 56
prophet 2, 58
prostitute 4
Proverb 16, 65
provision 14, 59
punishment 20
purified 16, 17
pursue 24, 31

Q

quarrelling 51
queen 40

R

Rabbath 36
Rachel 53
Rahab 4, 5, 15-17, 26
raiment 64
rebel 2, 42
redeemed 15, 16
refuge 28-30, 58, 59
Rehob 44
Rehoboam 39
reject 19, 48
remnant of the giants 36
repercussions 46, 51

responsibility 73
resurrection 58
Reuben 11, 63
Reubenites 64
riches 17, 64
righteousness 58
right hand 17
River 6, 9
Rock 68
rubies 16
rule 4, 7, 34, 36, 37

S

sacrifice 20, 23, 54
salvation 27
Samson 55, 58, 68
Samuel 58
sanctified 20
sand 32, 35, 68
Sarah 45
Saul 62, 69
save 16, 19, 34, 41, 59, 60
scarlet 5, 19
scribes 5
scripture 18, 23, 27, 37, 39, 46
sea 6-10, 12, 27, 28, 32, 35, 37, 68
seashore 32
separation 16
servant 1, 2, 7, 17, 23, 26, 27, 29, 58
serve 8, 34, 35, 46, 49, 54, 67, 71-73

sheath 69
Shechem 13, 25
sheep 18, 27
shekels 48
Sheshai 42-44
Shiloh 64
Shimron 32
Shur 38
Sihon 27, 29, 36
silent 17, 21
silver 15, 16, 18, 47, 48, 64
Simeon 13
sin 19-21, 56
sincerity 71
sing 65
slaughter 69
slave 10
smoke 33
snare 38, 39
sojourn 13, 45
Solomon 11, 46, 48
spies 5, 24, 42, 44, 60
spirit 2, 12, 20, 55
sprinkled 19
stamped 40
stature 36, 42
stone 9-11, 23
storage city 48
stranger 13, 59
strife 51
study 5

subdued 58

sword 13, 25, 34, 56, 67-69

Syria 48

T

Tabbath 68

Tadmor 48

Talmai 39, 42-44

temple 11

temptation 64

Terah 71

territory 56

terror 2, 27

testimony 30

Thamar 20

thread 19

throne 3, 62

Tirzah 50

travail 19

tree 17, 23

trembling 69

tribe 9, 11, 49, 51, 53-56, 61, 63

trodden 20, 60

trumpets 68

trust 30, 63, 69

truth 20, 71

twelve 9, 10, 44

twenty 26, 35, 39, 69

twin 18, 19

U

uncircumcised 13
   understand 16, 17, 61, 64, 65
   unholy 20

V

valley 18, 24, 28, 32, 33, 68
   vessels 16
   victory 17, 23, 32
   vile 30
   villages 58, 61

W

wages 64
   wait 21, 22, 24, 43, 57, 58
   walked 57
   wandered 41, 43
   war 11, 13, 17, 26, 28, 31, 34, 35, 56, 63-65
   washed 19
   watchmen 69
   water 6, 7, 9, 10, 12, 16, 19, 27, 33, 37
   weapons 35, 56
   wedge of gold 18
   weep 45
   wife 38, 39, 46, 47, 53, 61
   wilderness 13, 14, 35, 41, 43, 44, 48, 61
   wilfully 19, 20
   window 5

wise 2, 15-17, 23, 47, 65

witness 20, 63

woman 5, 15, 16

womb 19

wonders 2

works 43, 66, 73

worship 64

wrath 29, 63

Y

yarn 48

young 43, 65, 69

Z

Zarah (Zerah) 18-20

zealous 63

Zebulon 56

Zelophehad 50, 51

Zererath 68

Zin 44

Zoan 42

Zorah 55, 56

About the Author

Rob de Jongh is a lifelong Bible student and has been sharing his perspective on the Bible through talks, studies and group work for the last 20 years. He has written over one thousand Bible studies and has become known for his fresh perspective, accessible writing style, and ability to make the Bible relevant. He formerly worked as a non-fiction editor alongside some of the world's best educators, and helped to devise bestselling books for two successive publishers. Catch up with him at www.woodland.press

Printed in Great Britain
by Amazon